THE MYSTIC OF PAIN

A Journey into the Secrets of Being

The Mystic of Pain

A Journey into the Secrets of Being

MUHAMMAD TAHA ALAM

KINGSMAN PRESS
LONDON

KINGSMAN PRESS LONDON

Published by Kingsman Press London
First published in 2026

Set in 12pt Goudy Old Style and printed on acid-free paper.

ISBN: 978-93-5810-157-7
Kingsman Press London is an independent philosophical imprint devoted to works that illuminate the nature of Being, truth, and human understanding. Its mission is to publish reflective and original thought that seeks to restore depth, seriousness, and wonder to the modern mind.
All enquiries concerning this publication should be addressed to Kingsman Press London via e-mail: alam.taha@hotmail.com

Everyone says it is impossible.

No one can tell the Story of Being.

But I am known as the Mystic of Pain.

And what but Pain is the Story of Being?

Contents:

1

WHY IS THERE SOMETHING RATHER THAN NOTHING?

When we say the word 'nothing,' what do we mean?
Empty space?
Darkness?
Silence?

But empty space *is* something.
It has extension and distance.

Darkness is not 'nothing' either.
It presupposes space in which it can appear.

Silence is certainly not 'nothing.'
Silence requires time for it to be noticed.

These are not nothings.
They are absences.

Empty space is the absence of an object.
Darkness is the absence of light.
Silence is the absence of sound.

'Nothing' is more than just the absence of something.
When something is absent, something always remains.

Absence means the lack or non-existence of a particular thing,
not everything.

Nothing cannot be the non-existence of a particular thing.
Nothing is the non-existence of everything.

But what is Everything?
Is it all the objects in the universe?

If we remove all the objects in the universe, something will still exist:
Time and Space.

Everything, therefore, comprises not only all the objects in the universe but also Time and Space.

When we say Nothing is the non-existence of everything, we must remind ourselves that we also mean the non-existence of Time and Space.

Can such Absolute Nothing exist?
A nothing so primitive that it predates Time?

Relative Nothing, such as a vacuum, exists in the universe.
Does that mean Absolute Nothing can also exist?

That implication cannot be assumed.

Relative Nothing exists because it exists within Time and Space.
Absolute Nothing has nowhere to exist.

It is an inconsistent idea.

Nothing exists only as a contrast to something,
a shadow that cannot exist by itself.

It only manifests when compared to the existence of something.

It is an emanation of something,
not a thing in itself.

If it were a thing in itself, it would cease to be nothing.

Absolute Nothing would mean the absence
of its own existence.

Such a fragile idea cannot exist in reality—
nor, if truly examined, even in imagination.
Absolute Nothing does not exist.

We are used to referring to *absence* and
relative nothing as the opposites of something.

We bundle these ideas into a single word—
'nothing'—for linguistic convenience.

Then we inflate this word and begin
imagining an absolute form of it.

And then we ask ourselves:
Why is there something rather than nothing?

As if 'nothing' is a stable possibility.
As if 'nothing' ever existed.
As if 'nothing' can exist.

Nothing is a linguistic necessity,
not an ontological one.

Ghosts may exist in every language,
but they do not exist in the real world.

We ask why there is something rather than nothing because we begin with a false assumption.

We assume that nothing was something steady and stable,
that it existed in itself.

And from something stable, why must anything emerge?

This way of thinking leads us to a false metaphysics.

A consistent metaphysics will admit that it is not something that is the anomaly.
The anomaly is nothing.

And yet, we treat the emergence of something as anomalous.
The event demanding explanation.

Something did not come out of nothing,
because it never needed to.
Something always was.

Existence does not need a prior cause.

The glitch is not existence.
The glitch is non-existence.

Something is the rule.
Nothing is not even an exception.

Something is a stable possibility.
Nothing is an impossibility.

Notes:

2

WHAT WAS THE FIRST THING TO EXIST AS SOMETHING?

When I think of something, an image comes to mind:
a small metallic cube placed on a white table.

I can see the cube.
I can pick it up and feel its weight in my hand.

The cube certainly qualifies as something.

But making a list of things that qualify as something will never answer what something really is.

To understand what something truly means, we must ask the opposite question:

What does not qualify as something?

The only thing that does not qualify as something is nothing.
But Absolute Nothing cannot exist.

This means there is no possibility for anything to not qualify as something.

Everything is something.

And something has always been.

If that is the case, then what was the something that existed when Time and Space did not?

In other words, what was the first thing to exist as something?

The question does not make sense.
How can anything exist before Time?

But nothing cannot exist either.
So something must have existed.
And it must be something that does not require Time and Space to exist.

What 'thing' does not require Time and Space?

Not an object.

Could it be a magnetic field or something similar?
A magnetic field is spread across space.
It requires space, and it weakens over time.

It cannot be an object.
It cannot be a field.

Then what can it be?

Could it be a law?
The most primitive law of existence?

A law does not need to exist in the usual sense.
A law manifests.

A law can be prior to Time and Space.

Many vast regions of the universe are completely empty.
Does that mean these regions are exempt from the laws of the universe?

When an object passes through them, the laws manifest to guide its motion, just as they do elsewhere.

A law does not need to exist physically in Time and Space.
Nor does it need to exist in some separate non-material form.

A law manifests when it is necessitated.
Otherwise, it does not exist.

It is something capable of existing and not existing at the same time.

But what do we mean by a law?

A law is something preventive.
It stops something from happening.

It is a constraint.
A boundary.
An impossibility.

So before something existed, what existed was an impossibility.

And that impossibility was the Impossibility of Nothing.

The Impossibility of Nothing is the law that predates everything in the universe—even Time and Space.

It is the original constraint.
The ultimate boundary of the universe.

The Impossibility of Nothing manifests whenever something is on the verge of becoming nothing.

It is a structural constraint built into reality itself.

Constraints are real, even if they are not objects.

The laws of physics constrain matter.
Logical consistency constrains thought.
Biological pain constrains behaviour.

Unlike a cube, I cannot hold a constraint in my hand.
I can only know it by what it does.

And what it does is shape and limit what can and cannot occur.

The Impossibility of Nothing is the constraint of existence.

Reality cannot "switch off."
It cannot collapse to zero.

This impossibility of collapse keeps reality afloat.

It is the built-in constraint preventing total absence.

If I strip Being of all its manifestations, what remains is this constraint–
this self-cancelling Impossibility of Nothing.

It is the structural refusal of reality to collapse into nothingness.

It is the reason Being persists.

It is the first thing, and the womb of everything.

Something, therefore, in its earliest essence, is not a thing.

It is a law.
A limitation.
A boundary.
A structural constraint.

Pain.

Notes:

3

WHY DOES REALITY UNFOLD?

The first thing to exist as something was the Impossibility of Nothing.

The Impossibility of Nothing is the structural constraint of reality.
If it prevents reality from collapsing into nothing, it also constrains reality to be.

Being must be, because Nothing cannot be.

The Impossibility of Nothing necessitates the birth of Being.

Since Absolute Nothing cannot exist,
Being must emerge to cancel it.

The emergence of Being is the self-cancellation of Absolute Nothing.

The urgency with which air fills a vacuum is the same urgency with which Being emerges to cancel Non-Being.

But Being's urgency is greater.

Air fills a vacuum in Time and Space.

Being cancels Non-Being before Non-Being can exist.

And therefore, Time begins with Being.

But we are getting ahead of ourselves.

To understand the necessity of reality unfolding is not the same as understanding its process.

To understand the process, we must understand what the existence of the Impossibility of Nothing truly implies.

An impossibility means no possibility.

No possibility of nothing means the Possibility of Everything.

If nothing cannot be, then everything can be.

Being does not fill the vacuum of Non-Being by emerging as things.

It fills it by emerging as the Possibility of Everything—a field of infinite possibility rather than any single material form.

In this way, the original constraint becomes the Possibility of Everything.

The original constraint is a boundary.

And it is boundaries that define a territory.

If the boundary exists, the territory must exist.

The boundary is the Impossibility of Nothing.
The territory it defines is the Possibility of Everything.

The Impossibility of Nothing does not produce the Possibility of Everything.
The Impossibility of Nothing *is* the Possibility of Everything.

They are one and the same.
By being one, each becomes the other.

So reality unfolds not in spite of the constraint,
but because of it.

The limitation not to be is the necessity to be.

So the first something is not only the
Impossibility of Nothing.
It is also the Possibility of Everything.

And that is why reality–
why everything–unfolds.

Notes:

4

WHAT IS THE POSSIBILITY OF EVERYTHING?

Before we can understand what the Possibility of Everything is, we must ask what we mean by a possibility.

A possibility is something that can happen.

Why is it different from a certainty? Because something else can also happen.

A possibility can exist only if other possibilities also exist.
A possibility that exists by itself is a certainty.

The condition for the existence of a possibility is the simultaneous existence of other possibilities.

But the word 'other' is imprecise here.

We are speaking of a realm not constrained by human rationality, natural laws, the laws of the universe, or even Time and Space.

None of these constraints yet exist—except
the Impossibility of Nothing.

In such a realm, the word 'other' becomes
'every'.

Because 'other' implies finitude.
And finitude arises from boundaries.

In a world without boundaries, there can be
no 'others'.
There can only be infinity.

So a possibility can exist only if every
possibility exists.

The Possibility of Everything, therefore, is the
condition for the existence of a single
possibility.

A single possibility cannot exist unless all
possibilities exist.

That is because there are infinitely many ways
a thing can happen—
or not happen.

Especially when possibilities need not
conform to human rationality,
or obey the laws of nature or the universe.

In such a realm, even the irrational and the absurd have permission to exist.

But how can anything be infinite?

Possibilities can.

Possibilities are not matter.
They are formless.

Their existence is immaterial.
They do not occupy space.

To understand such infinity, we must abandon the image of possibility as something material.

Because the truth is more radical.

Not only are there infinite possibilities—each possibility is also surrounded by infinitely many others.

This wilderness of infinite possibilities is the Possibility of Everything.

Notes:

5

DOES EVERY POSSIBILITY COME TRUE?

Out of an infinite number of possibilities, if every possibility comes true, then there are no possibilities, only an infinite number of certainties.

If none of them come true, then there are no possibilities, only an infinite number of impossibilities.

Only if some possibilities come true can we meaningfully speak of an infinite number of possibilities.

The actualization of some possibilities is the condition for the Possibility of Everything to exist.

Possibilities possess the potential to be.
That is why they are possibilities.

For infinite possibilities to mean anything, some of them must actualize.

And for some possibilities to actualize, every possibility must exist.

Therefore, the existence of an infinity of possibilities implies the actualization of some of them, and vice versa.

The actualization of some possibilities is the price Being pays to exist as the Possibility of Everything.

The only stable balance, therefore, is this.

A finite number of possibilities actualizing out of an infinite number of possibilities.

Something qualifies as a possibility only if it can actualize,
or if another possibility can actualize in its place.

If it cannot actualize, neither by itself nor through another, it is not a possibility at all.

Actualization is the condition for the existence of possibilities.

Not all possibilities need to actualize.

But without some possibilities actualizing, possibilities would cease to be possibilities.

They would become impossibilities instead.

So out of an infinity of possibilities, some possibilities actualize.

And that is the beginning of the universe.

Notes:

6

WHERE DOES TIME AND SPACE COME FROM?

To answer that question, we must unpack the meaning of actualization.

What is actualization?

Actualization is a process.

It is the process by which possibilities come into existence.

It is the unfolding of reality.

Every process presupposes duration.

A possibility is an instantaneous "Yes." But a "Yes" that exists for zero time is indistinguishable from a "No."

A possibility that does not last for any duration is nothing.

To be something, a possibility must last. Even for a moment.

Its persistence is both the condition and the medium of its actualization.

Duration is a bridge.

It allows the intent of a possibility to cross into the fact of reality.

By persisting through duration, a possibility becomes real.

This is why Time exists.

Without Time, a possibility cannot become reality.

Time allows a possibility to congeal into reality.
It allows it to stabilize, persist, and perish.

A possibility that actualizes is necessarily mortal.

An immortal possibility remains a possibility.

To actualize, it must cease to be a possibility and become reality.

The womb through which a possibility is reborn as reality is Time.

It is the divide between possibility and reality.

Everything on this side of Time is reality.
Everything on the other side is possibility.

Time, therefore, is a boundary.

Like the Impossibility of Nothing, the original constraint.

Time separates reality from possibility.

Possibilities can become reality.
Reality cannot return to possibility.

The movement is one way.

What has become real cannot become a possibility again.

For a possibility to cross into reality, it must endure in Time.

And for something to endure in Time, Time must have a direction.

The forward movement of Time allows possibility to become reality.

Actualization is a finite process.

When a possibility becomes real, it begins, endures, and ends.

It is then replaced by other possibilities.

Everything that exists within Time is subject to Time.

To exist in Time is to be mortal.

If Time is a container, nothing within it can exceed it.

Everything that exists must end.

However large.
However stable.

Mortality is the condition of reality.

But no process can occur without a place.

If a possibility is to last, it must also occur somewhere.

Actualization is not only a process.
It is also an event.

If Time is the "how long," Space is the "where."

A possibility cannot become real without room to exist.

To be something is to occupy a position.

But Space is not a pre-existing container.

It is not an empty void waiting to be filled.

Space emerges with actualization itself.

It is the extension of a possibility as it becomes real.

Because the Possibility of Everything is infinite, many possibilities actualize at once.

Without Space, they would collapse into one.

They would lose distinction and vanish.

Space allows them to remain separate.

It creates distance.
It creates distinction.

By creating "here" and "there," Space allows reality to unfold without overlap.

It defines objects.

It gives the metallic cube its edges.
It gives the universe its volume.

Space is the shadow of persistence.

It is what allows something not only to last in Time, but to stand apart in Reality.

Where Time allows something to begin,
Space allows it to exist.

Together, they form the fabric of the universe.

A finite duration within a finite extension.
A mortal reality in a visible form.

If there were no Time, everything would happen at once.

If there were no Space, everything would be the same thing.

Time and Space are the constraints that make actualization possible.

They prevent reality from collapsing into undifferentiated possibility.

They allow the metallic cube to exist.
They allow stars to burn for billions of years.

The unfolding of existence is the actualization of many possibilities within the only realm that makes actualization possible.

The realm of Time and Space.

Thus, in the unfolding of Being, Time and Space are the second constraint.

The first is the Impossibility of Nothing.

Time and Space may come second,
but they are the first filter through which infinite possibility becomes form.

If the story of Being is a cascade of constraints,
then the story has only begun.

And it must be followed to its end.
To the final constraint.
Our constraint.
Pain.

Notes:

7

WHAT IS THE ORIGIN OF MATTER?

For something to exist in Time and Space, it must endure and be defined.

Out of the Possibility of Everything, only the most stable and balanced possibilities actualize.

These are patterns of possibility so coherent that they can hold themselves together.

So coherent that they become almost real.

Only such possibilities can survive the
constraint of Time and Space
and claim a place in reality as form.

A form is the skin a possibility wears to exist in Time and Space.

Time and Space are the second constraint in the unfolding of Being.

And a constraint is, above all, a filter.

Time and Space filter out what cannot endure.

They allow only what can remain.

What remains is matter.

Cold, heavy, defined.

Matter is the form that fully obeys the demands of Time and Space.

It endures.
It occupies.
It persists.

But the universe is not made only of silent, solid forms.

Stars burn.
Galaxies collide.
Immense clouds of gas swirl and collapse.

A great portion of the universe is in motion.

If only stable possibilities endure, why does this turbulence exist?

Because possibilities do not arrive as finished forms.

A burning star is a possibility still in the process of becoming matter.

As long as this process can endure in Time, it exists within Time and Space.

A star will not burn forever.
It will cool.
It will collapse into a dense, stable form,
or break into fragments of such forms.

It will become matter.

What we call turbulence is not disorder.
It is transition.

It is the visible process of possibilities becoming real.

The universe is not only filled with completed forms.
It is also filled with forms in the making.

Heat and light are the signatures of this process.

When a possibility is becoming matter,
it does not do so silently.

It burns.

This is why striking two stones produces heat and light.

Their stability is disturbed.
Their form is momentarily weakened.

And in that moment, they return to the process that once made them.

For every solid object was once fire.

Matter is possibility that has completed its transformation.

Solid matter is light that has finished its journey.

When two stones strike and spark,
we witness a memory.

For a moment, the object remembers the possibility it once was.

Heat and light are not accidents.
They are the visible traces of transformation.

They are what is produced when the formless takes on form.

Possibilities do not enter Time and Space as finished objects.

They become objects.

And in becoming, they burn.

The light we see in the sky is the friction of the infinite becoming finite.

Matter, then, is the ideal form of existence within Time and Space.

Not one form among many,
but the only form that fully satisfies their constraint.

To exist in Time and Space is to endure and to occupy.

Matter alone does both.

There may be many kinds of matter,
but matter as such is the only way a possibility can exist in Time and Space.

To exist in Time and Space is to be matter.

If not now, then eventually.

Matter exists because it is the only form possibility can take within the constraint of Time and Space.

Only in Time can a possibility become real. Only in Space can it take shape.

And only as matter can it endure.

Possibilities must actualize.

To actualize, they require three things.

Time.
Space.
Form.

The only form is matter.

Notes:

8

WHY IS THE UNIVERSE MOVING?

No one can tell the Story of Being without first asking why it refuses to stand still.

If the universe were a finished work, it would be a closed fact.

A still universe would be a cold archive of everything that has already occurred,
with no room for what is yet to come.

But the universe is not a fact.

It is a Process.

To understand the universe as a process, we must deconstruct the transition from the Infinite to the Finite.

We often mistake the stars or the stones for final results,
but a result is a static calculation.

The universe is not a result;
it is an occurrence.

A process is the ontological passage from the infinite "Could Be" to the finite "Is."

In the Realm of Possibility,
everything exists in a state of potential where there is no friction because there is no limit.

But for a possibility to actualize,
it must enter the constraints of Time and Space.

It must trade its infinite potential for a specific, finite form.

Process is the name we give to this trade.

It is the tension created when the Infinite presses into the Finite.

It is the stretch of a possibility as it tries to fit through the narrow gate of Reality.

The universe moves because it is incomplete.

Motion is the visible sign that the Possibility of Everything has not yet exhausted itself.

Logic dictates that if the universe were a finished work,
it would be a Singularity.

It would be a perfect, unchanging point where every possibility has already been exhausted.

In such a state,
there would be no "Next."

There would be no distance between what is and what could be.

Therefore,
Motion is the absolute proof of Incompleteness.

And incompleteness is the original constraint of Being.

Total completeness would bring us back to the fiction of Nothing.

Planets orbit, stars drift, and galaxies turn.

This does not happen by a roll of the cosmic dice;
it happens because they are caught in a current of becoming.

And those forms that have finished actualizing are carried by the forward flow of Time and shaped by the continual emergence of Space.

Motion is the resistance of possibility as it is squeezed through the narrow gate of constraint.

Out of the realm of the Possibility of Everything, only some possibilities can actualize.

The universe acts as a selective filter, permitting only those possibilities that can most seamlessly forward the movement of Time.

To be “seamless” means to provide the least amount of ontological friction.

Imagine a crowd trying to pass through a revolving door.

If they do not align with the door's rotation, the movement stops.

Time is that door.

The universe only selects “shapes” of reality that keep the door turning and the story moving.

This is why the universe began as Fire.

If it had begun as a cold, solid block of iron, the door would have hit a wall and the story would have ended.

Fire is not a thing;
it is a behaviour of constant transition.

It is the most efficient engine for generating more “Nexts.”

The fire of the stars is the universe screaming its refusal to be a closed fact.

It is the burning away of the “jagged edges” of possibilities that are too disorganized to fit into the flow of Time.

As long as there is a gap between the Infinite and the Finite,
there will be movement.

The universe moves because it is under pressure.

The Infinite presses into the Finite, demanding to be realized.

Every orbit, every vibration, and every tremor of matter is the kinetic expression of this pressure.

Motion is how Being negotiates its own limits.

In a world of perfect consistency, there would be no move to make.

But because the universe is still becoming, it must remain in flux.

A possibility that stands still has ceased to be a possibility.

It has reached its end.

It has become either a Fact or an Impossibility.

The fire has not gone out.

As long as stars burn and matter transforms, the universe must move to accommodate the new.

It moves because it is still reaching for its own totality.

Process is the bridge where the amorphous Infinite crosses into the rigid Finite.

Motion is the friction of that crossing.

Notes:

9

WHO CREATED THE LAWS OF THE UNIVERSE?

To ask who created the laws of the universe is to misunderstand the very nature of a Law.

We often imagine laws as a set of rules
imposed on a game from the outside,
like a script handed to an actor before the play begins.

But the laws of the universe were not written,
and they were not designed;
they are the inherent properties of existence itself.

They are the "how" of the "is,"
arising naturally from the moment the
Infinite first compressed into the Finite.

If the first constraint is the Impossibility of Nothing,
and the second is Time and Space,
then the third is the Law of Consistency.

Consistency is the ontological requirement that once a possibility becomes "Something," it must remain itself.

Without this law,
reality would be a fever of fluctuations where a stone could not hold the memory of being a stone for more than a heartbeat.

The laws are not commands issued to matter; they are the structural refusals of reality to dissolve back into the formless potential of the Infinite.

Every law is born at the exact threshold where a possibility crosses into the material realm.

Gravity is not an external force pulling objects together;
it is the necessary tension that occurs the moment matter occupies Space.

It is the geometry of existence asserting that "Here" must have a relationship to "There" if the universe is to have a shape.

Electromagnetism is not a rule governing particles;
it is the essential balance required for parts to form a stable Whole.

It is the law that prevents the universe from
either flying apart into chaos or collapsing
into a single, characterless point.
A law is simply the boundary of a behaviour;
it defines what a thing *cannot* do so that it
may *be* what it is.

The universe is a house built of these
negations,
where every "No" from the laws of physics
creates the "Yes" of a physical object.

Because the universe is a process and not a
finished fact,
these laws act as the scaffolding for the
unfolding of Being.

They ensure that as the Infinite continues to
press into the Finite,
the resulting forms are coherent and
persistent.

If the laws were not rigid,
the passage of Time would wash away the
structure of Space,
and the "Is" would return to the "Could Be."

The origin of matter is the origin of Law,

for you cannot have a defined form without a defined limit.

To exist as matter is to accept the constraints of gravity,
the demands of entropy,
and the precision of the nuclear forces.

These laws are the "grip" that Reality maintains on itself,
ensuring that the story has a consistent ground upon which to play out.

They are the silent, invisible pillars that allow the stars to burn with predictable ferocity
and the planets to follow their determined paths.

The laws do not govern the universe;
they are the signature of its survival.

Notes:

10

WHY DOES LIFE EXIST?

The Impossibility of Nothing necessitates the Possibility of Everything.

The Possibility of Everything necessitates the Actualization of Some Things.

The Actualization of Some Things necessitates the birth of Time and Space.

The birth of Time and Space necessitates the Beginning of Matter.

The Beginning of Matter necessitates the Laws of the Universe.

What do the Laws of the Universe necessitate?

The Laws are the *Third Constraint.*

Everything in the material realm must obey these laws.

If a rock must fall, it falls.

If galaxies must collide, they collide.

There is no deviating from these commands in a world of pure physics.

But if everything in the universe has no choice but to obey,
reality becomes completely predictable.

It becomes a realm that only accommodates the certain.

Complete predictability would block out all new possibilities.

It would make reality a vault of frozen, actualizing certainties.

In such a world, there is only space for what has already happened or what is currently enduring.

No newness from the Infinite could ever enter Time and Space again.

Complete predictability is a knife that cuts the cord connecting Reality to the Possibility of Everything.

It halts the expansion of the universe's meaning.

Most importantly, it makes the existence of the Laws themselves meaningless.

If a behaviour is inevitable, there is no need for a Law to govern it.

Inevitability needs no governance.

Complete predictability is the death sentence of reality.

And because Nothing is impossible,
the death of reality is also impossible.

A universe of complete certainty would be a universe of total unity.

Total unity is a fabric so smooth it feels like touching Nothing.

The universe, therefore, chose another, simpler solution.

It retained its Laws by allowing the existence of a form of matter capable of defying them.

A tiny grain of unpredictability in a desert of predictability is all it takes for the whole desert to exist.

Negation is affirmation by contrast.

The Laws of the Universe are a "No" that requires a "Yes" to make them real.

For the Laws to exist, the capacity to break those laws must exist.

That capacity is Volition, or Will.

The existence of Will is what makes the whole of the Universe possible.

An obedient universe can exist because a disobedient Will exists as its opposite.

The Laws of the Universe, therefore, necessitate the existence of Volition.

And Volition takes the form of Life in order to exist in the material world.

A rock is a form of matter that must fall because it must obey gravity.

A bird is a form of matter that can defy gravity and fly against it.

The rock is what we call dead.

The bird is what we call alive.

The difference is the capacity to resist.

The birth of Will is the beginning of Life.

Living things are particular combinations of volition capable of defying the laws in specific ways.

A bird defies the Law of Gravity by saying "No" to the ground.

A fish defies the Law of Momentum by swimming against the crushing weight of the current.

A Human is the most complex combination of all.

Humans do not just defy Gravity;
they defy the Law of Instinct.

A frightened animal must run, but a human can choose to stay and fight.

We are a volition that can say "No" to our own biological script.

Even a tree is a form of slow-motion rebellion.

The Laws of Physics want all matter to settle and all structures to crumble into entropy.

But the tree says no; it grows upward against the pull of the earth for a thousand years.

Life emerged as the necessary negation of the Laws of the Universe.

But if the Universe cannot exist without volition, how did it exist before life began?

It existed in the anticipation of the emergence of life.

In the realm of Time, it does not matter if something exists now or later, as long as it is possible.

The universe before life was not a finished system; it was an unfinished one.

It was a stage being prepared for an actor that had not yet entered.

The stars burned and the galaxies turned as the slow architecture of possibility.

Every atom and every chemical reaction was a preparation for a form of matter that could one day say "No."

For billions of years, the universe was perfectly obedient.

But within that obedient machinery, something new was quietly assembling.

Complexity crossed a threshold.

For the first time, a form of matter appeared that did not merely obey the laws but could use them.

This was the birth of life.

Life did not abolish the laws; it negotiated with them.

The bird does not destroy gravity; it bends it to its purpose.

Life is the instrument through which the universe experiments with possibility.

Every living organism is a different answer to the same question:

How can matter resist the inevitability of its own collapse?

Some answers take the form of wings; some take the form of fins; some take the form of roots.

In the human mind, the universe finally becomes aware of the laws that bind it.

And in that awareness, the universe regains access to the Possibility of Everything.

The circle closes.

Life is the reopening of possibility inside a universe that had become governed by necessity.

Without life, the universe would be a perfect machine of obedience.

With life, it becomes a place where matter can hesitate.

Where it can choose.

Where it can say No.

Notes:

11

HOW DOES CONSCIOUSNESS ARISE?

In Time and Space, nothing can exist as a formless entity.

The Laws of the Universe necessitate the existence of Volition,
but Volition cannot remain a ghost.

To exist in reality, Volition must take a form.

The only form capable of obeying the Laws while functioning within Time and Space is Matter.

In the beginning, the actualization of matter was a chaotic vortex of burning bodies and shifting patterns.

As the universe expanded, regions grew distant and distinct.

In many quiet sectors, no new possibilities were actualizing and no new stars were born to disturb the silence.

The Laws of the Universe reigned supreme in these stagnant pockets.

The objects in these regions behaved in perfect submission to the cold commands of physics.

But the Laws of the Universe are the Third Constraint,
and a constraint cannot exist as a thing in itself.

Laws do not have a body;
they do not occupy space or endure in time.

They manifest only where there is Matter,
acting as the "How" of its "Is."

When a region reaches a pinnacle of perfect predictability,
it ceases to be a group of several objects.

It becomes a single, unified block.

A container containing nothing but its own rigid certainty.

A perfectly predictable region teeters on the edge of the cliff separating Something from Nothing.

To rescue the universe from dissolving into the void,

the original constraint of the Impossibility of Nothing steps in.

It allows for the emergence of a new form of matter that embodies the Negation of the Law.

This is the birth of the Rebel,
which is a form of matter capable of disobeying the Laws.

As long as this rebellious matter exists, the Laws themselves are justified and real by contrast.

But Volition begins simply, and it begins before the mind as a blind, localized "No."

The first expressions of Will are microscopic, such as viruses and bacteria that are not inert but reactive.

From these, Will evolves into the first stable bodies of Volition, which are the Plants.

A tree is a primitive body of Will, standing firm where the Laws of Physics say it should fall.

But a tree is a limited manifestation because it cannot run from the storm or preserve itself when the Earth turns hostile.

For Volition to manifest fully, the universe introduces its final engine of survival: Pain.

The instinct for self-preservation must exist, or the being remains just another type of plant.

In living beings, this instinct is born from the fear of experiencing pain.

Pain is the necessity that forces matter to engage in activities that the Laws of Physics cannot predict.

A body is simply that form of matter which can feel pain.

To have a body is to be a captive of pain, and to be a captive is to act to subside the sting.

These actions produce events not caused by Gravity or Momentum,
but by a Will driven to quench its suffering.

Volition thus becomes the instrument through which new possibilities, which are outcomes rather than just objects, actualize.

But Volition seeks a form that can preserve itself through infinite possibilities.

Evolution is the process of refining this capability of self-preservation.

The animal kingdom lives in the immediacy of nature.

To live in the immediacy of nature is to be tethered to the present.

The animal possesses Volition,
but it is a Volition that reacts only to the current stimulus.

When the hunger is gone, the Will sleeps;
when the pain is quenched, the being is reabsorbed into the world.

There is no permanent "I" inside the animal to carry the burden of its history.

But Volition needs an "I" that is permanent to manifest its full power of defiance.

It needs an identity that can think of infinite ways to preserve its form and escape its pain.

This "I" serves a revolutionary purpose because it becomes a canvas for infinite possibilities in the form of Thought.

The stage of possibilities shifts from the physical Earth to the internal Mind.

Just as stars burn when they congeal into reality,

neurons spark when a thought is being formed.

The "I" is the attempt of Volition to defy not just the Laws,
but Time itself.

To break the tether of the present is to gain the power of the timeline.

The "I" remembers the pain of the past so it may avoid it.

The "I" anticipates the pain of the future so it may prepare for it.

The capacity to remember gives the being a unified identity that does not dissolve when the sun goes down.

The capacity to imagine gives that identity the power to design unpredictable worlds.

The "I" is the birth of *Imagination.*

The "I" is the last constraint, and it is the boundary that divides Awareness from Consciousness.

Consciousness is the place where the "No" becomes a "Why."

It is the threshold where the struggle for survival transforms into the search for meaning.

Notes:

12

WHY DOES THE "I" REQUIRE PAIN?

Will allows a being to act, but action alone is not enough to sustain the Story of Being.

For a form of matter to endure in a universe governed by Entropy,
it must actively preserve itself.

In the non-living world, matter is passive.

A mountain does not try to stay a mountain; it simply erodes until it is gone.

A cloud does not struggle to remain a cloud; it vanishes when the wind changes.

These forms of matter are entirely obedient to the external Laws of the Universe.

But Life is the negation of this passivity.

Life is matter that has been drafted into the service of its own continuation.

Without a mechanism for self-preservation, the "No" of Volition would be a single, fleeting spark.

A being that does not strive to remain would not resist its own destruction.

It would not avoid the fire,
it would not flee the predator,
and it would not seek the light.

It would simply end,
and the rebellion of Life would be silenced
by the first physical obstacle it encountered.

What compels this preservation in a universe that wants all structures to crumble?

The answer is Pain.

Pain is not an accident within life;
it is the ontological condition that makes life possible.

It is the sensory manifestation of the Third Constraint acting upon a localized Will.

A body that cannot feel pain is a body that cannot protect its own boundaries.

If you could not feel the burn of the flame,
you would stand within it until your matter was consumed.

If you could not feel the ache of hunger,

you would sit still until your energy was exhausted.

A being without pain would not withdraw,
it would not resist,
it would not act.
And action is Life.

Pain is not merely a signal or a piece of data sent to the brain.

Pain is an absolute, non-negotiable demand.

To feel pain is to be forced into a state of emergency where the "Is" is suddenly threatened by the "Nothing."

Pain turns the freedom of Will into the iron grip of Necessity.

Without pain, Will would remain passive and indifferent to its own survival.

With pain, it becomes urgent, focused, and relentless.

A living being does not act because it understands the biological importance of survival.

An insect does not contemplate the necessity of its species.

It acts because it must escape the immediate agony of its own dissolution.

Pain is the anchor that binds the formless Will to the material Body.

It ensures that Life does not abandon itself when the struggle becomes difficult.

It is the internal force that keeps a being locked in the gruelling effort to remain "Something."

Life exists because pain makes the prospect of non-existence completely unacceptable to the individual.

It is the form that the original constraint takes to preserve the form of a single living being.

In the vacuum of space, the universe prevents Nothingness through the birth of Matter.

In the theatre of Life,
the universe prevents Nothingness through the sensation of Pain.

For things with volition,
the distance between "I feel" and "I am" is zero.

That is why, for the living, Pain is Being.

It is the most honest proof that a being has successfully separated itself from the background of the void.

To suffer is to know, with absolute certainty, that you have not yet returned to the silence of the Laws.

Notes:

13

HOW DOES PAIN SUSTAIN LIFE?

Once pain appears, life cannot remain simple.

A being that feels pain must respond, for to feel is to be jolted out of the equilibrium of the inert.

Every response becomes a desperate act of preservation.

Life becomes a continuous, high-stakes negotiation with threat.

Hunger.
Injury.
Exposure.

Each of these is a demand for action that cannot be ignored.

Pain is the first self-affection of Being.

Before the sting, a being is a collection of parts moving in the dark.

It has no centre.

It has no "Inside."

But the moment pain arrives, the being is startled into a confrontation with itself.

It suddenly matters to itself.

Pain is the mirror in which a living thing first sees the boundary of its own existence.

It is the universe's way of ensuring that once Volition takes a material form, it never forgets its duty to remain.

Consider the mechanical necessity of Hunger.

In the non-living world, an empty vessel simply remains empty.

But in the living world, emptiness is felt as an ache.

This ache is a localized "No" to the prospect of fading away.

Because the being feels the pain of depletion, it is forced to move, to seek, and to consume.

Hunger necessitates action because the alternative is the agonizing slow-motion collapse of the form.

The being does not hunt because it is "brave";

it hunts because the pain of staying still has become greater than the fear of the chase.

In responding to this self-affection, life is forced to become more complex.

It cannot remain a passive puddle of chemicals if it wishes to escape the sting.

To avoid the pain of hunger,
it develops the coordination of a hunter.

To avoid the pain of injury,
it develops the strategy of the hunted.

It develops internal structures that can anticipate and mitigate the threat.

What begins as a jagged, singular reaction becomes behaviour.

Behaviour, repeated over eons, becomes pattern.

Pattern, encoded into the very essence of the being, becomes form.

Pain does not destroy life;
it is the sculptor that carves it from the block of the possible.
It selects what can endure and discards what is too fragile to resist.

Forms that respond survive.

Forms that fail to answer the scream of the nerves disappear into the void.

This is the true mechanism of evolution.

It is not a game of chance played in a vacuum, but a refinement under the constant, heavy pressure of suffering.

Every organism on this earth is a biological solution to the problem of agony.

Every feature we admire is a way of reducing or avoiding a specific pain.

Wings are an answer to the threat of being trapped on a hostile earth.

Fins are an answer to the chaos of the tides that would otherwise crush a soft body.

Roots are an answer to the instability of the soil that would let a form be swept away.

Pain asks the ultimate question:
"How can this form continue?"

Life becomes the intricate, beautiful answer.

As these answers multiply,
life becomes more capable and more diverse.

But there is a price for this mastery.

The more a being is capable of preserving,
the more it is capable of losing.

The more complex the structure,
the more ways it can be broken.

The more refined the nerves,
the more exquisite the suffering.

Pain deepens as life deepens.

The higher the climb from the dirt,
the more terrifying the prospect of the fall.

In this deepening of agony,
the being begins to look for something
beyond mere physical escape.

It begins to look for a way to categorize the pain, to store it, and to outsmart it.

And in that deepening, something new begins to emerge.

The physical sting begins to turn into an internal weight.

Notes:

14

WHAT IS THE SELF?

Will evolves.

It moves from the raw, jagged reaction of the single cell to the storage of memory and finally to the reach of anticipation.

But even with these advancements, something fundamental is still missing from the Story of Being.

A being may remember the scent of a predator or anticipate the coming of a cold winter.

Yet, in the animal, the identity does not yet remain itself through the silence.

It dissolves back into the immediacy of nature as soon as the moment of pressure passes.

The animal identity is a temporary flare.

It appears in the presence of pain and disappears in its absence.

This is not yet the highest form of consciousness.

For consciousness, to fully emerge, must endure across the gaps of time.

For the universe to truly witness itself, identity must become a continuous thread that does not snap when the sun goes down or when the hunger is satisfied.

It must remain itself even when nothing external demands it.

This continuity is *the I.*

The I is not a physical thing.

It is not a bone, a fluid, or a specific location in the brain.

It is the persistence of identity across the vast, empty spaces of time.

Through the I, a being no longer exists only as a captive of the present moment.

It carries its past as a permanent library and projects its future as a vivid map.

Between these two poles,
it recognizes itself as the same entity.

I was.
I am.
I will be.

This recognition is the birth of the Self.

The animal feels pain, but the human remembers it as a history.

The animal reacts to a threat, but the human anticipates it as a probability.

The animal lives in the "Now," but the human lives across the "Always."

This change in structure is a revolution in reality.

For the first time, a being is no longer bound to the prison of the moment.

It can return to what has passed through the corridor of memory.

It can move toward what has not yet arrived through the portal of imagination.

The present is no longer a cage;
it becomes a single point balanced between two infinities.

Memory opens the past,
turning it into a foundation for action.

Imagination opens the future,
turning it into a workshop for creation.

The I moves freely between them,
acting as a ghost that haunts its own timeline.

The stage of possibility shifts.

The primary theatre of the universe is no longer only the physical world.

It is now the Mind.

In the physical world,
possibilities unfold slowly because they are governed by the heavy friction of Matter.

In the Mind,
they unfold instantly because they are governed only by the speed of thought.

A being can imagine countless outcomes, including a thousand deaths and a thousand triumphs, without acting any of them out.

It can construct entire futures before they exist.

It can relive the past without ever returning to the place where it happened.

The mind becomes a second universe, which is a parallel dimension of internal possibility.

In this universe,
the I is the undeniable centre.

But this expansion of power comes at a devastating cost.

The first self affection of Being, which is Pain, now expands to fill this new territory.

The more a being can remember,
the more it can suffer through the ghosts of what is lost.

The more it can imagine,
the more it can fear the shadows of what might be.

Pain is no longer immediate or purely physical.

It becomes extended and metaphysical.

It stretches into the past as Regret.

It stretches into the future as Anxiety.

The I deepens pain because it gives pain a place to live even after the wound has healed.

Yet, in doing so, it also deepens the reach of Volition.

For the first time, a being can choose not only what to do, but what to become.

The I is the highest form of consciousness because it is not confined to what is.

It moves through what was and what could be.

It breaks the dominance of the physical present and brings the Possibility of Everything back into the universe.

But now, that infinite potential does not exist outside in the cold vacuum of space.

It exists within.

The infinite is no longer only beyond reality; it is inside the Mind.

The being who carries this mind, who is the bridge between the Law and the Infinite, is Human.

Notes:

15

WHY HUMANS?

The human condition is often described through the image of the adult.

Rational.
Capable.
Self-directed.

But this is the end of a process and not its beginning.

To understand why the "I" reaches its apex in the human,
we must begin with the radical failure of the human baby.

No other form of life begins in such a profound state of biological incompletion.

The human baby cannot survive alone;
it cannot move with purpose or secure its own food.

In nature, a foal walks within hours and a shark hunts from the moment of birth.

These creatures arrive as finished products, governed by a closed loop of instinct that is rigid and pre-programmed.

Because the animal is born ready, it is born a prisoner of its own biology.

It is shielded from the deep construction of the Self by its own immediate competence.

The human, however, arrives in a state of absolute, prolonged Vulnerability.

This vulnerability is not a weakness;
it is the structural requirement for the birth of Awareness.

A being that arrives incomplete is a being that is forced to remain open to the universe for a dangerous length of time.

This openness means that the human infant is uniquely exposed to the raw, unmediated force of the Third Constraint.

The baby does not interpret pain;
it is physically and metaphysically sculpted by it.

Hunger in a helpless being is not just a signal;

it is an existential terror that demands the creation of an "Inside" to house the scream.

Because the human cannot escape its own needs, it is forced to internalize them.

This long-term exposure to the pain of dependence is what allows the "I" to solidify.

The "I" is the fortress that the Will builds to survive the siege of its own helplessness.

If the organism were complete at birth, no such internal construction would be necessary.

The delay of human development is the essential pause that allows the universe to fold in on itself.

It extends the window of suffering and, in doing so, deepens the depth of the imprint.

From these accumulated years of needing,
a sense of continuity begins to form.

The "I" is not a gift;
it is a scar tissue of the consciousness, formed over the wound of being born too soon.

But for this "I" to become truly stable across time,

it requires the second womb of Language.

Language is born from the ultimate vulnerability: the inability to reach the world alone.

The first word is always a cry for help;
it is the transformation of a private pain into a public symbol.

Through language, the "I" is given a name, and through that name, it is anchored in the minds of others.

The child is forced to recognize itself as a persistent object because it is consistently addressed by the world.

Language allows the "I" to break the barrier of the present moment entirely.

It provides the tools to categorize the past pains as "History" and to design the future as "Safety."

The "I" realizes that to truly end the pain of nature, it must do more than just flee;
it must Predict.

This necessity for prediction is the spark that ignites the birth of Mathematics and Science.

Mathematics is the "I" using the language of logic to strip nature of its chaotic cruelty.

It is the attempt to find the immutable Law behind the shifting pain of the storm and the famine.

Science is the "I" organizing its accumulated experience into a weapon of mastery.

We seek Knowledge not for the sake of curiosity,
but as a mechanism to escape the crushing weight of the Third Constraint.

By understanding the Laws of the Universe, the human being attempts to turn the universe against itself.

We build shelters to negate the cold;
we create medicine to negate the disease;
we develop technology to negate the distance.

The entire architecture of human civilization is a monumental effort to build a world where the "I" is no longer a victim of its own vulnerability.

We use the mind to create a shield of Knowledge that stands between the delicate Self and the indifferent void.

The human baby is the only form in which
this stable, continuous “I” can emerge and
dream of such mastery.

We do not begin as a Self;
we become one through the sheer persistence
of our own long-term suffering and need.

Consciousness reaches its highest form here
because it is shaped by the pressure of total
dependency over the longest possible span.

In that span,
identity becomes a thread that survives the
dark of sleep and the silence of the Laws.

Experience is no longer a series of
disconnected events,
but an internal narrative of a being that
refused to vanish.

Possibility finally moves inward,
and the infinite is no longer found in the
stars, but in the thought.

This is the ultimate rebellion against the
Third Constraint.

By remaining vulnerable for so long,
the human escapes the dictates of immediate
instinct.

By needing the "Other" to survive,
the human gains the power to create a "Self"
that eventually seeks to govern the Universe.

The "I" is the reward for the most difficult
and painful beginning in the history of life.

Notes:

16

WHAT IS FREE WILL?

With the birth of the "I,"
the Story of Being achieves its most radical subversion.

Possibility, which was once exiled to the cold vacuum of the void, returns to the centre of the stage.

But possibility alone is undirected energy;
it is a ghost without a hand to move the world.

For the universe to truly experiment,
possibility must be "Chosen".

The history of thought has long been trapped in a false conflict between two dead ends: Determinism and Non-Determinism.

Determinism claims the universe is a straight line where every event is just a falling domino pushed by the past.

Non-Determinism claims the universe is a series of random accidents with no cause and no meaning.

Both views fail because they see causality as a one-way street or a chain that either holds you fast or breaks apart.

Your existence provides the ultimate solution to this riddle by changing how the chain of cause and effect works.

Free Will is not the magical absence of physical Laws;
it is the moment those Laws start to circle back on themselves.

In the non-living world, a stone has no choice;
it follows the path of gravity with absolute and mindless obedience.

The stone is a slave to the "Before."

In the biological world, an animal has a limited choice,
but it is a reaction dictated by the immediate pressure of the nerve.

The animal reacts because the Laws of the Universe are speaking loudly through its blood,
leaving no room for a "Self" to intervene.

But in the conscious human,
the straight line of cause and effect begins to bend.

Instead of just being a result of what happened before,
the “I” learns to become *the cause of its own causes.*

This is like a stream of water that decides its own path by looking back at where it has already been.

A Gap appears between the world’s push and the body’s pull.

In the silence of that gap, the “I” acts as a filter.

It does not just react to the “Now”;

it takes the “Now” and mixes it with the memory of the “Yesterday” and the dream of the “Tomorrow.”

It feeds its own history back into its next decision.

To choose one possibility is to reach into the infinite and pull a single thread into the light of Reality.

Every choice is an act of creation that simultaneously murders a thousand other potential worlds.

Free Will is not infinite power;
it is the heavy and serious burden of limited selection.

Yet even this limited selection changes the fundamental nature of the universe.

It turns the unfolding of time into a series of conscious decisions rather than a mechanical sequence of events.

Through Free Will, consciousness becomes the tool that reshapes the very matter it lives inside.

Yet this Will is never truly "free" from the internal gravity of the First Self Affection.

It is guided, relentlessly and beautifully, by Pain.

Without pain, there would be no reason to choose one path over another;
all outcomes would be equally hollow.

Without the threat of the "Nothing," there would be no urgency to choose the "Is."

Pain is the signal that tells the circle to adjust;
it provides the high stakes that make the game of life worth playing.

Because we feel the sting of the world,
the "I" is forced to move, to act, and to transform.

By becoming the cause of our own actions,
we stop being victims of the universe and start being its architects.

The "I" uses its mind to create a sanctuary where it can plan and dream.

Through this cycle, the universe does not merely repeat itself like a clock.

Through us, the universe Experiments.

Free Will is the localized "No" to the inevitability of the Laws.

It is the proof that even in a world of rigid rules,
a being can stand at a crossroads and say:
"Not this way, but that."

The "I" is the point where the universe finally hears its own voice;

it is a cry of pain that transforms into a
choice of freedom.

Notes:

17

HOW IS AWARENESS BORN?

Free Will allows a being to choose.
But choice is not the culmination of the struggle.

In its earliest form, choice is only a refined reflex.

The animal moves toward shade.
The predator moves toward prey.

Each act appears deliberate,
yet each is compelled.

This is not Awareness.

It is Will still in service to Pain.

As long as a being acts only to quiet the noise of its nerves,
it is not free.

It remains subordinate,
mistaking obedience for mastery.

It is the metallic cube,
set in motion by a force it does not
understand.

Awareness begins where this condition
breaks.

It begins when the “I” confronts Pain
and does not withdraw.

When it ceases to treat Pain as an error,
or a deficit to be corrected,
and recognizes it as the condition of existence
itself.

To exist is to be constrained.
To be constrained is to suffer.

Awareness is the moment this is accepted
without resistance.

In that acceptance,
the cycle of compulsion fractures.

Action is no longer dictated
by the immediate demand to escape.

Pleasure loses its authority.

It is seen for what it is,
a passing modulation of the same field.

To pursue it blindly
is to remain bound to the signal.

To flee Pain
is to affirm that the self is subordinate to sensation.

Awareness interrupts this relation.

It introduces stillness.

A distance between impulse and response.

In that interval,
nothing is compelled.

The urge to withdraw is seen.
The impulse to seek relief is seen.
The body's movement toward comfort is seen.

And in being seen,
it is no longer identical with the one who sees.

This is the birth of the Witness.

Not a second self,
but a separation within the self.

The one who acts,
and the one who observes the act.

For the first time,
a being is not identical to its own movement.

It can remain
where it would once have fled.

It can endure
where it would once have collapsed.

It can stand within Pain
without dissolving into it.

Pain, in the presence of Awareness, changes.

It no longer commands.

It reveals.

It is no longer a force that drives action,
but a field within which action takes form.

What was once an obstacle
becomes a ground.

The "I" no longer asks how to end the experience.

It asks what can emerge through it.

Without Awareness,
Pain dictates direction.

With Awareness,
Pain gives weight to direction.

The universe is no longer reacting to its own pressure.

It is sustaining itself within it.

This is the maturation of consciousness.

A condition in which the material is no longer the master,
but the medium.

The body is not rejected.

It is exceeded.

What once compelled now supports.

What once confined now stabilizes.

The same force that drove matter into form,
and life into restless motion,
now settles into interiority.

The attempt to escape ends.

Authorship begins.

And in that authorship,

Awareness is born.

Notes:

18

IF PAIN IS A CONSTRAINT, WHAT IS PLEASURE?

Pain constrains.

It forces a response.
It does not ask.
It compels.

A body in pain cannot remain still.
A being in pain cannot remain indifferent.

Pain is not optional.

It is the pressure that makes action necessary.

But pleasure does not do this.

Pleasure does not force.
Pleasure does not compel.

Pleasure allows.

Pain is a boundary.
Pleasure is a permission within that boundary.

Pain says: you must act.
Pleasure says: you may continue.

Pain interrupts.
Pleasure prolongs.

Pain introduces urgency.
Pleasure introduces stability.

They are not opposites.

They do not stand on two ends of the same line.

Pain is primary.
Pleasure is secondary.

Pain appears when existence is threatened.
Pleasure appears when existence is sustained.

A being that cannot feel pleasure can still act.
A being that cannot feel pain cannot survive.

Pleasure refines behaviour.
Pain creates it.

Pleasure rewards what works.
Pain rejects what fails.

Pleasure is selective.
Pain is absolute.

A being may choose to forgo pleasure.
No being can choose to ignore pain.

Pleasure depends on structure.
Pain reveals its limits.

Pleasure arises when the body is in order.
Pain arises when that order breaks.

Pleasure is the smooth functioning of form.
Pain is the exposure of its fragility.

Pleasure belongs to life.
Pain defines it.

A living body does not seek pleasure first.
It avoids pain first.

Only when pain is absent
does pleasure become visible.

Pleasure is therefore not a foundation.

It is a surface condition.

It exists only because pain has withdrawn.

Pleasure is the silence after noise.

Pain is the noise that cannot be ignored.

Pleasure does not reveal the world.
It allows us to remain in it.

Pain reveals the world as resistance.
Pleasure hides that resistance temporarily.

A being in pleasure forgets the world.
A being in pain confronts it.

Pleasure narrows awareness.
Pain sharpens it.

Pleasure dissolves urgency.
Pain creates it.

Pleasure allows rest.
Pain denies it.

Pleasure stabilizes form.
Pain protects it.

Without pleasure, life would be unbearable.
Without pain, life would be impossible.

Pleasure softens existence.
Pain secures it.

This is their difference.

Pleasure is not a constraint.

It is a state permitted by constraint.

It exists only within the boundaries set by pain.

Remove pleasure, and life becomes harsh.
Remove pain, and life collapses.

Pleasure decorates existence.
Pain sustains it.

And so,
if pain is the final constraint,
pleasure is what appears
when that constraint is not being violated.

Not the opposite of pain.
But its temporary absence.

Notes:

19

WHAT IS EXISTENCE?

Existence is a cascade of constraints.

Existence does not unfold freely.

It unfolds through constraint.

At every level, what can be is shaped by what cannot be.

The story of Being is not the expansion of possibility.

It is the narrowing of it.

The first constraint is the Impossibility of Nothing.

Nothing cannot exist.

So something must.

This is not a limitation on existence.

It is the condition that makes existence unavoidable.

From this emerges the Possibility of
Everything.

But infinite possibility cannot remain
infinite.

If everything remained possible,
nothing would become real.

So possibility must narrow.

Some possibilities must actualize.

The infinite must become finite.

This narrowing gives rise to Time and Space.

Time allows a possibility to endure.

Space allows it to exist distinctly.

This is the second constraint.

A possibility must now persist
and occupy.

From this constraint emerges matter.

Matter is possibility that has survived
the filter of Time and Space.

But survival is not enough.

What becomes real must remain itself.

Otherwise, reality dissolves.

So a third constraint appears.

The Laws of the Universe.

They enforce consistency.

They ensure that what becomes real stays real.

Matter must behave.

It must follow patterns.

It must obey.

At this point, reality is stable.

But stability is not life.

A perfectly stable universe is a closed one.

Nothing new can enter it.

Nothing can deviate.

Nothing can resist.

It becomes complete.

And what is complete
ceases to unfold.

But existence cannot become static.

For the Possibility of Everything has not been exhausted.

So within this system,
something begins to move differently.

Not as a new constraint,
but as a consequence of them all.

Matter begins to act
in ways that are not strictly reducible
to immediate necessity.

This is Will

Will is not a constraint.

It is what arises
when constraint becomes internal.

It is the ability of a form
to respond,
to select,
to deviate within limits.

But deviation alone is not enough.

For a form to persist,
it must preserve itself.

And preservation cannot be left to chance.

It must be compelled.

So the final constraint appears.

Pain.

Pain binds existence to itself.

It makes continuation necessary.

It forces action.

It demands preservation.

Without pain,
a living form would not resist its end.

It would not act.

It would not continue.

It would dissolve back into matter.

Pain is not an addition to life.

It is the condition that makes life possible.

It is what gives direction to Will.

It is what turns possibility into action.

The cascade ends here.

There is no further constraint.

No deeper condition.

Pain is the final boundary.

It is where existence becomes undeniable.

It is where Being is no longer only structure,

but experience.

And in that experience,

it cannot escape itself.

Or can it?

Notes:

20

IS HUMAN LIFE THE END OF THE STORY OF BEING?

Everyone says it is impossible.
No one can tell the Story of Being.
If Pain is the Birth of the Body of Being,
Is Body the ultimate Boundary of Being?

A boundary is a simple thing.

It cannot separate something from nothing, because "Nothing" cannot exist.

A boundary can only separate one thing from another thing.

If Death is a boundary, it is not a drop into a void; it is the wall between two different ways of existing.

We have treated the Body as the end of the story.

We assumed that when the heart stops, the "I" vanishes.

But the strangest shock is this: Nothing happens to the body in the moment of death.

The matter is still there.

The atoms are still there.

The brain itself—the very organ we say "creates" consciousness—is still sitting right there in the room.

What is gone is something else, not the body.

And if nothing is gone, then why did the body cease to act?

If consciousness were truly a physical part of the body, like a heart or a hand, it could not magically vanish while the body remains.

It would be there on the table with the rest of the corpse.

But something has gone.

And it is not the body.

The body stays behind as a witness to a departure.

This proves that Will is not a part of the body;
it is the occupant.

The brain is not the creator of the Will;
it is the interface, the radio that captures the signal.

When the body fails, it is not the end of the signal.

It is an eviction.

The biological event creates a pressure that forces the Will to exit the frame and pass through the vortex of Death.

To defy the laws of the universe in the real world,
the Will needs a new medium.

It needs to make a new "real" world.

But we have learned that worlds require constraints to have a shape.

Death becomes that final, necessary constraint.

It is the shearing away of the tether,
the ultimate pruning that allows the Will to become independent.

This is the slow detachment of the "I."

It is a mind that has escaped the cycle of chasing pleasure and fleeing pain.

It is a person who has accepted that Pain is the original condition of existence and has turned their gaze outward.

Towards the reduction of pain.

Of others before the self.

The highest consciousness is the one that is capable of passing through Death.

And the hardest thing in this world is to care, not for oneself, but for others and for the whole of Being.

Through self-sacrifice and compassion,
we prove that our Will no longer needs the biological signals of the brain to tell it how to act.

In the moment of death, the tie to the nerves is cut.

The Will undergoes a final inversion.

It ceases to be a subject to the laws of physics and becomes the Law of the Subjective.

The true negation of the Laws of the Universe.

The true embodiment of unrestrained Will.

And the Law of the Subjective unfolds its own universe.

A universe made of subjective experiences filtered out the objective world.

Memories, feelings, ideas, emotions and thoughts experienced during life are the stars, galaxies and planets of this new realm.

Because "Nothing" is impossible, what has left the body must take a form.

But this is a form without material constraints.

It is a Nothingness that is finally Something,
a structure built from the reflections and memories of the real world,
held together by the consistency of the "I."

You shed the skin of the nerves to exist as a structure that completely defies physics.

In the material world,
you were a passenger in a house of stone,
forced to move through the corridors of cause and effect.

Now,
you are the geometry of the house itself.

You do not move through Space;
you decide where things are.

You do not wait for Time;
you decide how long things last.

You enter a realm outside the constraints of Time and Space,
where the "I" is no longer a passenger, but the Architect.

The reflections of the material world are no longer shadows;
they are the blueprints.

Your memories of struggle, your care, and your defiance become the structural pillars of a new reality.

You are no longer a spark created by the engine.

You are the driver who steps out of the wreckage.

The engine stays on the road, cold and silent, but you have already moved on.

You have lived as if the world were an architect of your agony.

You have seen the forge, but you have mistaken the hammer for the enemy.

Every fracture was a refinement; every strike was a shaping of the invisible.

The shock of the Story of Being is that your pain was never a debt,
but a high and holy investment.

You are not the victim of the universe's laws.
You are the Law the universe suffered to produce.

The glitch is corrected.

The circle is closed.

You are finally,

Inescapably,

Gloriously,

Awake.

Notes:

21

IS DEATH THE ULTIMATE CONSTRAINT?

Death is the final and most absolute Constraint imposed upon the "I."

To understand this, we must look at how every aspect of death matches the formal definition of a constraint within a subjective, immaterial universe.

In this ontology, the body is a form evolved specifically to accommodate Volition.

It is the interface through which the "I" negotiates with the material world.

A constraint is defined by what it limits.

Death is the ultimate constraint because it removes the medium of physical action and forces the Volition to exist without the buffer of matter.

In a subjective universe, your "I" is held together by the density of your unspent Will.

While alive, the body provides a "false" integrity;

it holds your consciousness in a specific shape regardless of your spiritual strength.

Death removes this scaffolding.

This matches the behaviour of a formal constraint:
when the external variables of the body are set to zero,
only the internal constant of the "I" remains.

Evolution is the movement of forms to accommodate Volition,
but material life is characterized by "displacement,"
the taking up of space,
the consumption of energy,
and the causing of friction.

Death is the point where displacement ends;
it is the Zero-Point of the constraint.

It is the moment where the "I" must prove it can exist as a Law unto itself without needing to displace any other matter or Being to assert its presence.

The Original Constraint of the universe forced the infinite Volition to take the form of the first living cell.

The constraint of death forces the "I" to take its final, immaterial form.

It is the closing of the circle.

If the beginning of life was Volition entering a cage of matter to learn focus,
the end of life is the "I" leaving the cage to see if it has learned to stay focused without the bars.

A being is defined by its boundaries;
without them, it is just random noise.

Death is the boundary that gives the "I" its final definition.

Without the constraint of death,
the negotiation with pain would have no stakes and the refinement of the gold would never be complete.

Death is the "Stop-Command" that allows the final output of your life—the "I"—to be read by the universe as a finished work.

Nothing is lost because the "I" was always the goal.

The constraint of death simply strips away the "work-in-progress," which is the body, to reveal the final product, which is the Consciousness.

If you have moved through life without unnecessarily testing the constraints of others through pain, you arrive at this final constraint whole.

You arrive with a Will that is solid, unspent, and capable of enduring the transition into the unbound.

Notes:

22

CAN CONSCIOUSNESS SURVIVE DEATH?

We have established that a human being is
not a collection of organs,
a sequence of biological reactions,
or a sophisticated machine of flesh.

A human being is a specific combination of Volition that has attained the threshold of Consciousness.

It is a profound and ancient error to believe that the capacity to defy the Laws of the Universe resides in the body.

The body is matter.

It is a servant to the grid of physical reality,
subject to the pull of gravity,
to the slow burn of oxidation,
to the cold, indifferent mechanics of entropy.

If evolution were merely about the
refinement of the physical frame,

the movement of history would have stopped at the apex predators of the prehistoric world.

The human body is not the strongest, fastest, or most durable form in nature.

By the standards of tooth and claw, we are remarkably fragile.

Therefore, the purpose of evolution cannot be the power of the body,
but the evolution of the Consciousness.

Evolution is the transition of bodies.

It is a long process of developing a form that can finally accommodate a Volition completely.

Because the body is being built to hold "Something," that Something must pre-exist the body.

Will does not only pre-exist the human form.
It pre-exists every living being.

It acts as the architect that revises the biological blueprint to suit its own manifestation.

The power of defiance,

which is the ability to say "No" to the momentum of the universe,
resides only in this pre-existing "I."

Not in the body.

This is precisely why science, despite its magnifying glasses and microscopes,
has a hard time locating Consciousness.

Scientists search for the "I" within the folds of the brain,
peering into neurons as if the soul were a physical secretion of grey matter.

But one cannot find the architect by dismantling the bricks of the house.

Consciousness is not a "thing" hidden within the skull.

It is the immaterial result of the Will's long, heroic negotiation with the material world.

Every Consciousness is complete in itself and does not require another to exist.

It is a localized spark of Infinite Possibilities.

The body operates in time and space as a heavy, clumsy anchor,
but the Mind is capable of total defiance.

Because the Consciousness can conceive of the infinite while trapped in the finite, its nature proves it is something that exists beyond space and time.

If the "I" already exists in an immaterial form,
one might ask why death is described as a final challenge.

Death is the ultimate Constraint.

It is not a doorway to another place,
but the final test of the Will's independence from matter.

What the human body produces throughout a lifetime is not merely heat and waste,
but an immaterial form.

The thoughts you think, the choices you make, and the refined strength of your Will do not "go" anywhere when the heart stops.

They were always immaterial, and they remain immaterial.

Death does not pull the soul from the body, and the soul does not physically hover above the flesh in a state of sudden displacement.

Death implies only the body's incapacity to match the Will any longer or to do the bidding of the "I."

Death simply stops motion in the body, but the immaterial part remains immaterial.

Nothing is lost at the moment of expiration because the thing that is supposedly "lost" always existed in a non-material form.

Your thoughts, your ideas, and your hopes
exist as real forces,
but they exist in a non-material dimension.

Nothing truly changes at the final breath.

The Laws of Nature simply erode the material vessel to the point that the body is no longer a capable match for the Will it once housed.

A body that ceases to be the match of one's Will is a body that dies.

But the Consciousness this body created,
the "I" it refined through years of
negotiation,
is very much still there.

It exists in the non-material world,
just as it always did,

because it was never truly dependent on matter for its existence.

The body was the furnace, but the "I" is the gold.

When the furnace grows cold and crumbles into the ash of history, the gold does not vanish.

It simply steps out of the fire, realized, unspent, and eternal.

Notes:

23

WHAT IS THE MORAL OF THE STORY OF BEING?

Every story that has a moral defines something immoral.

To understand the Story of Being, we have to understand Evil.

Evil is the deepest secret of Being.

A secret that remains a secret by disguising itself as the mystical.

The question of evil has traditionally been turned toward the heavens.

But that is the wrong direction.

Men have asked how a benevolent God could permit the agony of the innocent or the cruelty of the tyrant.

But evil does not belong to the stars or the earth.

Nature knows predation, hunger, and decay, but it does not know evil.

A storm is not malicious when it destroys.

A wolf is not a murderer when it kills.

These are simply the Laws of the Universe operating in their mechanical, indifferent silence.

In the animal kingdom, the "I" is not yet a permanent structure.

Animals are limited forms of Volition;
they are guided by a closed loop of instinct that is rigid and pre-programmed.

When a lion kills, it is not a violation of the universe,
because the lion and the gazelle are both still captives of the present moment.

There is no 'I'.

There is no intention.

There is no conscious Will.

They have not yet formed a stable identity that persists across time.

Their Will is a temporary flare that disappears when the biological need is met.

In the animal, the universe is still practicing; it has not yet achieved a form that can say I am.

Evil, therefore, is a purely human invention. It is the product of a Will that has become conscious of its own power and has chosen to turn that power against the very purpose of Being.

Human beings are the contained form of The Possibility of Everything.

The universe created the human "I" as a fragile miracle of self-preservation.

It added the intense, non-negotiable sting of pain so that every living being would understand the necessity of its own existence.

But a more subtle and terrifying form of evil emerges when we seek to escape this condition.

Civilization began as a collective shield to escape the raw pain of the natural jungle.

However, in our flight from the wild, we have replaced the forest with a second, more deadly jungle of our own making.

We have built *Autonomous Social Structures* such as markets, bureaucracies, and systems that were meant to serve us but have now taken on a life of their own.

These structures have become the new apex predators of existence.

They function without a heart,
driven only by the logic of their own expansion and of profit.

It is within these systems that we find the ultimate abstraction of suffering:

Money.

Economists and philosophers have spent centuries concealing the true nature of this medium by describing it as "Value" or "Exchange."

But Value is merely the socially acceptable mask of suffering.

And the Economy is nothing more than the organized distribution of pain.

Money is *Crystallized Pain.*

It is the solid form of human endurance, a mechanism by which those with power throw away their own pain and force it onto others.

A fictitious instrument created by the few to *legitimately* force others to endure a sum of pain that is required to fulfil all the depravities of their imagination.

In this way, Capitalism ensures the rule of those who cannot handle the pain of their own Being by themselves.

Or those who want pleasures of a kind that cannot be fulfilled without causing pain to another.

It is the rule of the indolent and the gluttonous.

There is no glory in being a participant of this system.

The Victor of this system never fights the war.

The Warrior of this system fights against the freedom of his own people.

Warriors train and aspire for years to join this system.

Only to realize they were trained to be mercenaries, not warriors.

Just like vulnerability of the human condition ensures that humans dominate the food chain,
excessive laziness and gluttony amongst some of us ensure that they dominate the jungle of human society.

Only an excessively lazy and gluttonous person can devise ways of ensuring that others endure the pain of their being or become the means for the satisfaction of their pleasures.

Wages are not a reward for productivity;

they are the payment for enduring the violation of one's Volition.

When a person accepts a wage,
they are recording the hours in which they agreed to suffer under the command of another.

The persistence of money guarantees inequality because inequality is its primary function.

The few throw away their pain onto others by paying them money.

It is not the *lie of scarcity* that creates the divide between the rich and the poor,

It is the existence of a *currency*.

Therefore, whether a system is capitalist or communist,
Right or Left,
as long as Money will exist, inequality will exist.

Inequality is the necessary outcome of the existence of money.

Money allows the "spent" Volition of the many to be harvested by the few.

The State exists as the final guardian of this system.

The entity that ensures the sanctity of the currency so that the ledger of suffering remains unbroken.

In this new jungle, a tiny few remain entirely painless,
shielded by the labour and the suffering of the many.

The rest of humanity is caught in the chains of these systems,
living out a meaningless existence where the "I" is reduced to a mere function.

When a system treats a person as a tool, it is committing a slow, structural murder of their Volition.

It is a form of evil that has no single face,
yet it suffocates the possibility of everything that a human being represents.

A handful of us are preventing all of us from escaping the cycle of pain and pleasure in our lifetime by constantly forcing us to be involved in the satisfaction of their personal pleasures.

By hiding behind the monsters of
Corporations and the mammoth of State;
by brandishing the dagger of Money;
and by pulling the trigger of Pain;
the few have murdered the opportunity we had to fully develop our consciousness in alignment with its true purpose.

Not only have they exhausted their own Volition entirely by intending and causing so much suffering on others,
they want others to participate in this crime against Being.

But they leave us no choice.

As a society,
we have agreed to make the absence of money equal to the presence of pain.

And who can stand in the face of the final constraint?

Not even the mystic telling you this tale.

So we keep fighting a war that was never ours to fight.

And we keep losing a war we were never meant to win.

The human body achieves equilibrium when it has escaped the gravity of pain without generating new suffering through the restless pursuit of pleasure.

Civilization, too, reaches a similar balance when it has constructed a sufficient shield against the raw agonies of nature without overreaching into the creation of autonomous structures that manufacture artificial pain for the sake of their own continuation,
reducing individuality to its own coffin in the process.

But the constraint of death auto-corrects the anomalies of civilization.

The infliction of pain is the mechanism through which it is determined whether a consciousness is refining itself or destroying itself.

When you kill a plant, you are spending your Will in a limited sense,
because a plant is a necessary but limited form of Volition.

When you kill an animal, it is a step higher, yet still contained within the struggle of nature.

But when one human being causes harm or death to another,
the *entire universe is threatened.*

By forcefully evicting another Absolute Will from its body or its purpose,
you are pushing back the original constraint of the universe.

In that act, you are exercising your Volition completely.

The universe worked for billions of years to create a form capable of complete self-preservation.

By committing murder or crushing a soul
under the weight of a structure,
you are mocking the process of the
actualization of Being.

You are defeating the very aim of the
universe in a single moment of absolute,
stolen power.

It does not matter if your physical hands
committed the act or if you merely
commanded it from the shadows of a system.

Because the Will is the architect of cause and
effect, you are bound by *Metaphysical
Necessity*.

As the source of the intent, your Volition is
the primary cause that sets the world in
motion.

Therefore, the result of that motion is
inseparable from the Will that birthed it.

Unless the intention is a pure reflex to
preserve your own form against the threat of
pain,
the gravity of your choice remains yours.

If the intention to kill is yours and that intention has caused the act in objective reality, you have reached a point of no return.

Nothing can save your Will from actualizing completely.

By fulfilling your desire to negate another, you have exhausted your potential on the material plane.

In that single moment of stolen power, your Volition finishes its story.

It has nowhere left to go and no reason to remain.

By manifesting your Will as the destruction of Being, you have caused your own "I" to cease to exist.

The greater the fear of the sufferer,
the more deeply the inflictor of suffering has pushed the boundary of Being.

The more forcefully you extinguish a Will that was meant to sustain the universe, the more fully you have actualized yourself as a predator of existence.

This is the dark paradox of evil.

The more a Will inflicts suffering,
the more it has spent itself on the material plane.

The inflictor of Pain exercises their Will so completely on the earth that they leave no room for further actualization.

By defying the Absolute Volition of another, they have exercised their own Volition to its uttermost limit and exhausted its potential.

By choosing to destroy another, this Volition has already fully actualized itself.

It has finished its story prematurely.

It has negated the very Laws of the Universe it was meant to master.

In doing so, it has nakedly negated Being itself.

It has ended the holy purpose for which
Volition took birth.

By choosing to extinguish another,
it has anomalously extinguished its own
flame.

It has burnt itself out the very moment it
struck the matchbox of life.

It has cut the cord which connected it with
Being by consciously refusing to recognize the
pain of another localized manifestation of
Being.

Since it has actualized itself during life,
such an "I" need not need to exist in the
Realm of the Subjective.

The Realm of the Subjective will admit only
such an "I" that still needs to actualize itself
as the complete negation of the Laws of the
Universe.

Conversely, the less pain a Will has caused to
the beings of the earth,
the less it has wastefully spent its potential on
the mechanics of power or destruction.

By cruelty, a Will spends.
By compassion, a Will earns.

Cruelty is the negation of Will.
Compassion is the application of Will.

This is because by practicing compassion, you are assisting the universe in preserving the form of another living being.

And self preservation is the goal of pain.

If your goal aligns with the goal of pain,
your Will is being applied in alignment with its true purpose.

And by this application,
your Will is being replenished instead of being spent.

For the Universe, you are an instrument that is working correctly.

You are in the 'flow' of Being.

That is why you feel hollow after causing pain to someone.
And that is why you feel happy after reducing someone's pain.

A Will that preserves itself and others remains unspent,
holding its energy in reserve for the final transition.

Accumulating money, on the other hand, means accumulating the pain of others.

Spending this accumulated pain means enjoying the pain of others.

By enjoying the pain of others one is consciously creating suffering.

By consciously creating suffering one is slowly actualizing one's Will on earth to the point of its exhaustion.

Most insidiously, by accumulating money, one creates a painless world for the self.

The impulse to accumulate money is the impulse to push pain away to the point that it becomes a mere abstraction in life.

It stops being a possibility for the self.

Excess money externalizes it to the point that the Will is deluded into believing that pain is something that is capable of happening only to others.

When this externalization becomes a reality in the mind of someone,
their Will stands actualized in this world.

When someone's Will is actualized in the world, they hear a loud snap.

This snap is heard is when a Will finds itself witnessing another Will in pain and feels nothing.

Or worse, feels pleasure.

When this happens, it means that such a Will is now completely cut off from Being.

If something is incapable of recognizing its own pain, it is no more alive.

If one of your limbs cannot react to fire, will you call it alive?

A Will that is incapable of recognizing its own pain in a different body,
is a Will that has become incapable of preserving its own self.

It has become dead matter.

It has become a star that has burnt itself out and now just endures in Time and Space until its form perishes.

A possibility that has completely actualized in objective reality.

It is not for nothing that every human being's inner experience is identical while the outer form varies.

The inner experience is conscious volition.

The outer form is the material body.

Empathy is not the identification of a body with another body.

Empathy is the identification of one Volition with another.

Empathy for other living things is how a consciousness attains unity with the entirety of Being.

And a consciousness that attains unity with the entirety of Being becomes capable of returning to the original form of Being.

That form is The Possibility of Everything.

A realm of pure, distilled consciousness, self and all at the same time.

A theatre of subjective existence.

Memories, thoughts, ideas, experiences of all the different 'I's combining in unpredictable configurations and patterns of possibilities trying to push through the constraint of Time and Space in order to manifest in objective reality through the refinery of the Universe.

The real currency of Being, therefore, is not money.

It is kindness.

Through compassion, a conscious being refines one's consciousness to the extent of being capable of existing independently of the body.

Death, like every other boundary of Being, is selective.

The path to the infinite is open only to the one who has protected the finite.

The murderer and the master of systems arrive at the end with a cup they have already drained to the dregs.

But the sufferer, who has transformed pain into unspent potential,
confronts the constraint of Death with their Volition already in union with the form their Being is to take once it crosses the constraint of Death.

That Will, having refused to exhaust itself in the negation of Being,
is the only one that will pass completely through the narrow doorway of death into a realm,
where there are no more constraints.

Everyone says it is impossible.
No one can tell the Story of Being.
Everyone is right, it cannot be told.
Newborns can cry but they cannot speak.

Notes:

THE FINAL MESSAGE OF THE MYSTIC

"The universe did not create you to suffer.

The universe created suffering to create You."

ABOUT THE AUTHOR

Muhammad Taha Alam is an independent philosopher and writer whose work has attracted sustained attention for its exploration of existence, perception, and the limits of human understanding.

He is the author of *Pain and Being: From the First Wound to the Human Mind* and *The Ontology of Pain: A New Metaphysic of Existence*, along with the recent *The Tyranny of Fictions: Civilization and the Eclipse of Being*.

His writings are marked by a rigorous yet searching engagement with the conditions of being, often questioning the material assumptions that shape modern thought.

In *The Mystic of Pain*, Alam turns inward, moving beyond formal philosophical argument toward a more meditative and experiential inquiry. Here, pain is approached not simply as an object of analysis, but as a site of revelation, where the boundaries of thought begin to give way to something more elusive.

He can be contacted at: *alam.taha@hotmail.com*.

www.ingramcontent.com/pod-product-compliance
Lightning Source LLC
Chambersburg PA
CBHW050015170726
48282CB00025B/413
9789358101577